PROLOGUE

My name is Sally Comet, and I live with my parents on the famous spaceship the Gold-Wing.

Mum and Dad are archaeologists. They fly all around the galaxy looking for ancient treasures and forgotten things. Whatever they find ends up in the planet-sized museum Historia.

You've probably never seen anywhere like Historia. Every last centimetre of this planet is covered in awesome alien artifacts of every variety. It's chock-full of towering buildings, statues, art and other things that... well, even I don't really know what they are! I could spend my whole life exploring this museum and still not see everything there is to see.

When I am not wandering round Historia soaking up the sights, I get to go with Mum and Dad on all their adventures. I've travelled to a lot of different planets in my life. Big planets, little planets, planets covered in strange plants and even stranger animals... You name it, and I've probably chased it, run away from it or taken a photo with it. My favourite part of our trips is getting to meet

so many special and unique people.

I always learn something amazing, wherever we go. There was the time we met the wandering people of the planet Tartus. They taught me lots of great songs and how to throw my voice so that it seemed like I was in another room.

And of course, there were the lizard people of Cormac 5. They taught me how to move like a shadow, silent and invisible. Every day on the Gold-Wing is an adventure, and that's exactly how I like it.

Of all the adventures I've been a part of, my most exciting adventure so far took place on a tiny little swamp planet in the middle of nowhere. It all started in the control room of the Gold-Wing...

CHAPTER 1

A SUSPICIOUS SOS

"Sally!"

Mum called me to the front of the ship. She was hanging halfway out of one of the control panel hatches, practically  buried in cables and other important-looking electrical bits. Her hands were full of wires and tools, and she had a screwdriver tucked behind her ear.

"What?" I said, scurrying over.

"Flick the switch on that panel over there for me, would you? Then type the override code into your tablet – it's 5508. Just got to demagnetise the receptor coil and we should be back up and running again, but I need the power off first. I just can't reach it from down here." I followed Mum's instructions and hit enter on my tablet. The lights all around the control centre powered down with a soft hum. Mum adjusted something deep inside the panel. I had no idea how she knew which bit of that tangled mess needed fixing, especially in the dark. But just like always, with a few tweaks and drills, the panel whirred back to life again after a few moments. Someday I wanted to be as good at solving problems as Mum was.

"There," said Mum, as I helped pull her up to her feet. "Job done. Our communications deck should be good as new again."

A loud beeping noise crackled out from the freshly fixed communications deck. I knew that sound. That was a distress signal from a nearby ship. Someone was in trouble.

Dad hurried into the control room with us and flipped the receiver switch. The big viewscreen at the front of our ship lit up, and a large, alien face flickered onto the display. I had seen aliens plenty of times, but I'd never seen one with an eye-patch before, never mind two. Luckily for this alien, he still had one more eye. It boggled at us between the eyepatches.

The alien's voice burst through the speakers. "Argh, what a relief! Finally, someone has found us. My name is Captain Boggle-Eye Bill, and this is my scurvy crew, L.I. Ken and Slithe."

I had never seen any creatures quite like these guys. Ken was green, gangly, and entirely made of plants. I could hear him rustling as he leant over to wave at us through the screen. Slithe couldn't have been more different to Ken. He was pink and blobby like a jelly. He wore a sailor's bandana tied around the top of his head. While they seemed polite enough on the viewscreen, something didn't seem quite right about this odd crew.

The captain carried on. "Our ship broke

down and we were forced to land on this horrible swamp planet. We are in terrible trouble. Would ye be so kind as to lend a hand to such helpless travellers as we?" He clasped his hands together as he waited for our decision. Well, one hand and one glowing laser hook.

"I suppose it wouldn't take us too much out of our way," Dad said, starting to punch in the coordinates of the distress call.

"But what about our cargo from the planet Deshret?" I butted in. I had a bad feeling about these guys, but I couldn't quite put my finger on the reason why... Something about their outfits... the hook, the eyepatches and the sailor's bandana... "We've got to make sure that all that treasure makes it to Historia safely," I said. At the word 'treasure', the Captain's eye lit up.

"Our cargo can wait," Mum said, reaching for her toolkit. "If there's one thing more important than looking after historical artefacts, it's looking out for people in trouble."

"We'd be happy to help," Dad told Boggle-Eye Bill. "We'll be there in a flash."

"What kind, kind people ye are," the alien said. He leant back, turning to the two crew members behind him. "Ken, Slithe, say thank ye to

14

our kind rescuers."

"Yar, Captain. Thank ye, kind rescuers," chimed the two.

Dad swung the Gold-Wing in the direction of the small brown and green swamp planet. "Sally,

 your mum and I have to help these nice men out. We won't be long. You can wait here and do your homework if you like."

As my parents followed the coordinates of the distress signal, I made up my mind. My homework could wait. Something fishy was going on here, and I was going to get to the bottom of it.

CHAPTER 2

AHOY THERE!

My lizard friends on Cormac 5 had taught me well. As far as Mum and Dad knew, I was safe and snug on board the Gold-Wing. Little did they know, as they sloshed through ankle-deep mud, snapping twigs and rustling through tangled leaves and vines, I was right behind them all the way, silent and stealthy.

The dark, twisted tree trunks and heavy curtains of plant life made excellent cover. There were plenty of gnarled tree roots jutting out of the muddy water, and as I hopped between them,

any accidental noise was disguised by the croaks, buzzes and bellows of the swamp's alien life. I followed closely, all the way to the crashed ship. A glimpse of something white painted on the side of the ship caught my eye. It was covered by a drooping tree branch.

"Ahoy there," called the captain, waving at my parents with his laser hook. "We're so glad ye found us. Welcome aboard. Take as long as ye need."

My parents stepped into the ship with the strange crew. As soon as I was alone, I snuck closer to get a better look at the paint. I reached out, pulled the branch back, and...

A skull and crossbones. Oh no.

This could only mean one thing: Pirates! All at once, everything made sense. The 'argh's, 'yar's and 'ye's... the hook hand and the eye-patches... Mum and Dad were in serious trouble.

Just then, I heard a heavy squelching and the clanking of boots on metal. The pirates were coming out. I dashed behind a rock and hid.

SNAP!

I stepped on a twig. Immediately, all three of

the pirates stopped in their tracks and peered into the swamp.

"Cap'n, did ye hear that?" Ken asked, scanning over the bushes around me. I held my breath.

"Aye, t'was over there, by that rock." The captain squinted his one eye as he searched for the source of the sound. His laser hook crackled.

Uh oh. There must be some way I could... Wait! I had an idea. I closed my eyes and thought back to my time on planet Tartus. I took a deep breath, filled my lungs with air and let out a great big **"OO OOO OOO, AA AAA AAA!"**

I stayed frozen as my call echoed out from the branches of a big tree at the edge of the clearing.

All three pirates turned their heads towards the spot where I had thrown my voice. "Hmmph. Just a monkey," said the captain, lowering his hook. "Pesky things."

Phew.

With their attention no longer focused on me, the pirates huddled close to each other. I strained my ears to listen.

"Argh, they didn't suspect a thing. You are so smart, Cap'n, luring them in with a distress call," said Slithe, his whole body wobbling as he chortled.

"Now we can rob their ship while they're busy fixing ours," Ken added. He rubbed his leafy hands together in excitement.

This was bad. Our cargo hold was full of

golden artefacts, delicate ancient scrolls and other precious items from Deshret... even a sarcophagus! If we didn't get our cargo back to the Historia Museum, we wouldn't just lose a bit of sparkly treasure. We would lose thousands of years of important history.

Captain Boggle-Eye Bill grinned a toothy grin. "Let's go and see what booty we can find on their ship. They said it was called the Gold-Wing. With a name like that, we're about to be rich!"

CHAPTER 3

PIRATES AT THE HATCH

There was no time to warn Mum and Dad. The pirates were already making their way through the swamp with surprising speed. Ken seemed right at home here, surrounded by so many trees and bushes. The captain followed close behind, slicing through any obstacle that got in his way with his laser hook. Even Slithe managed to slide along without a problem. As I looked closer, I realised that Slithe wasn't just slipping past the thick undergrowth... he was sliding through it all!

Branches and twigs and rocks (and a few unfortunate frogs) slopped into Slithe's globby body,

only to plop out again as he wobbled on.

They were making quick time. If I wanted to have any chance of saving the Gold-Wing's precious cargo, I would have to sneak in round the back before the pirates had the chance to break through the main hatch.

At the Gold-Wing, the pirates got to work, prodding and poking at the hatch with their tools. Thankfully, they weren't quite as good at getting through doors as they were at getting through the swamp. Slithe kept accidentally slurping tools into his belly, and Ken had to stop fiddling with the lock every five seconds to bat Boggle-Eye Bill's oversized pirate hat out of the way. They might have been pirates, but at least they weren't smart pirates.

A plan was forming in my mind. If I could

put it into place before they broke in, I might have a chance to save the cargo. While the pirates were busy squabbling at the main hatch, I swiped my keycard at a side-entrance and headed for the Gold-Wing's storeroom. The storeroom was where we kept all of the equipment for the archaeological digs.

I grabbed a tablet, some standing lights and some really thin wire, then dashed down to the control room where I had helped with the power less than an hour ago. There were an awful lot of buttons, switches and dials in the control room, but I knew exactly which one I needed, all thanks to Mum. I flipped a switch, then sprinted straight to the cargo hold.

The pirates could break in any minute. I had to be quick.

CHAPTER 4

LIGHTS OUT!

I could hear the pirates breaking in as I worked, scraping and zapping at the lock. I tweaked a few wires and pushed the mummy back into the sarcophagus. A long screechy sound, probably the laser hook slicing through the door, was followed by a **CLUNK** and some very pirate-like cheers. They were in. I pushed the last light into place with my foot. *Bring it on, pirates.* I was ready.

The hatch door slid open, revealing the pirates. "Arrgh, we're in. Take a look at all this booty!" the captain said. All three of them were practically drooling over the crates of ancient treasure that we had loaded in from Deshret just two days ago. All around the hold were finely-crafted sceptres, jewelled statues and heaps of glittering coins.

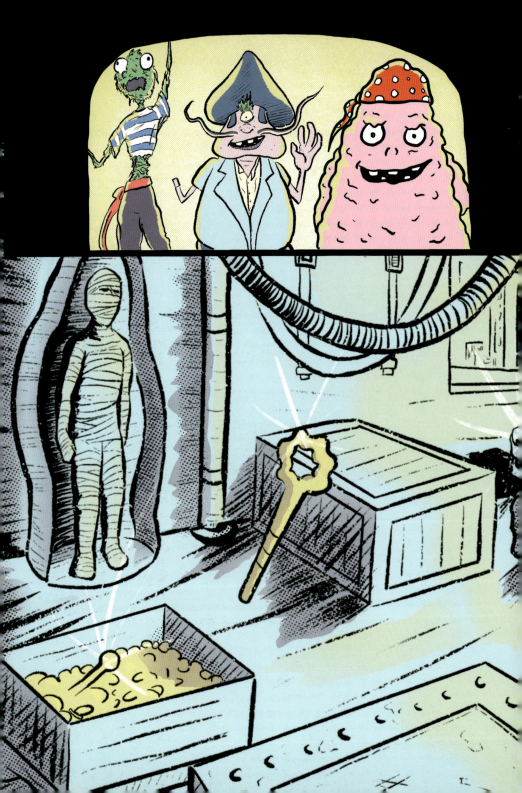

Ken scooped up a handful of coins and tossed them over himself. They showered down like golden hail, clattering on the ground around him. "We're rich, we're rich, we're rich!" Ken sang, leaping around. A few of the coins plopped into Slithe's jelly body, which made him giggle.

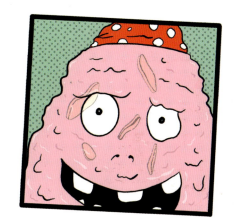

"Quick, lads, grab what you can!" said the captain, making a beeline for a sceptre.

That's enough of that. A few taps of my tablet – 5 5 0 8 – and every last light in the large cargo hold blinked off. The words 'OVERRIDE CODE ACCEPTED' flashed onto my screen. Thanks, Mum!

Darkness fell. The pirates gasped.

TAP TAP TAP. Standing floodlights beamed through the black, straight into the startled faces of the thieves.

Time for another trick. Opening my throat wide and low, I threw my voice across the room:

"WHO DISTURBS MY SLUMBER?!"

The pirates screamed. I tapped again. Another light pierced the darkness, lighting up the Sarcophagus of Secrets – and the terrifying mummy inside. I threw my voice again, louder.

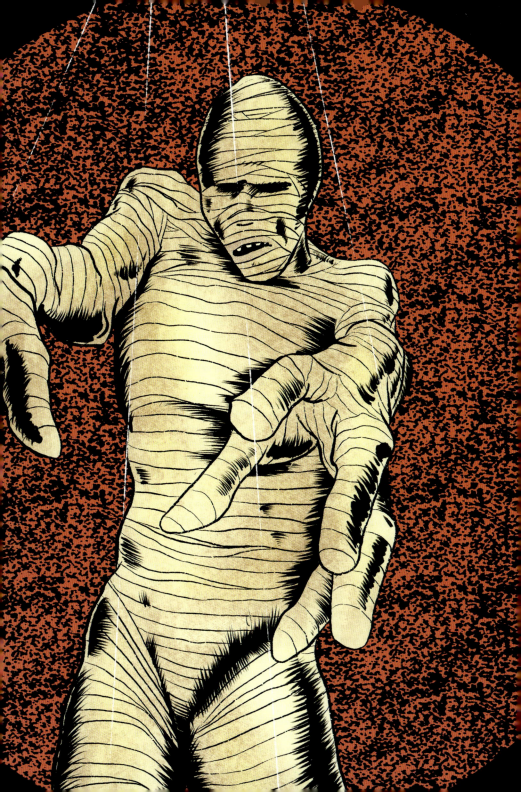

"WHO SEEKS MY TREASURE?!"

I tugged on the wires. The mummy's hands twitched. I yanked hard, and the mummy lurched out of the case and sprang towards the stunned intruders. **"I am the great pharaoh, Varden Kar the Third. BEWARE, all those who seek my treasure. An eternity of suffering awaits any who take my treasure from me!"**

Boggle-Eye Bill's bravery melted away instantly, and he dropped to his knees. "Forgive us, great pharaoh. Drop the loot, boys. Let's get out of here!"

Before the captain could finish his sentence, the entire

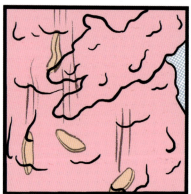

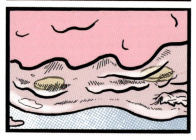

contents of Slithe's stomach spilled out onto the floor with a **SPLOOSH**. Gold coins pinged off the cargo hold floor.

"I don't want to be rich anymore, I don't want to be rich," Ken babbled as he turned on his heels and dived towards the exit hatch.

The pirates turned tail and ran from the Gold-Wing, tripping over themselves in their rush to escape. Boggle-Eye Bill's feet flew out from under him as he dashed full speed into a puddle of Slithe-coloured slime, and he slid uncontrollably across the hold floor... straight into the doorframe! The captain scrabbled to his feet again and dashed off into the swamp without even stopping to pick his hat up.

And just like that, the pirates were gone.

CHAPTER 5

A HASTY EXIT

I dropped the wires, huffing and puffing. The ancient mummy flopped down to the floor, as did I. That thing was heavier than I had thought it would be. "You know, we make a pretty good team, Varden Kar. Historical artefacts saved? Check. Pirates scared off? Check. Cargo hold secure? Well..."

I looked around. There were gold coins, gems and pink slime absolutely everywhere. My little show with the pharaoh had left the hold in a bit of a mess, but at least our precious cargo was all here and not in the pockets of those greedy space pirates that were sprinting back to...

Oh.

I jumped to my feet. Mum and Dad were still out there, and Captain Boggle-Eye Bill and his crew were heading right their way! I dashed out into the swamp again, following the trail of broken branches, muddy footprints and pink slime that the pirates had left in their wake.

I caught up to the fleeing thieves just in time to see my parents step out of the freshly repaired vehicle.

"Ah, gentlemen," Dad called out. "Perfect timing."

"It wasn't hard to fix," said Mum. "I found some leaves and pink gloop in the controls – hey!"

Ken rushed past my mum, babbling something about ghosts as he disappeared into the ship.

"You really
need to stop using
your laser hook to
steer," said Dad
as Boggle-Eye
Bill burst into
the clearing and
scrambled up the

plank to his ship. "I glued the pieces back to – hey,
watch out!" Dad dodged as Slithe, screaming and
wobbling, nearly slithered right through him.

Puzzled by the pirates' odd behaviour, Mum

and Dad watched
as the ship rattled,
rolled and roared
into the air.

"Wait, the hangar door is still open... never mind." Mum turned to Dad. "Wasn't that weird?"

I stepped forwards, forgetting completely that I was supposed to be on the Gold-Wing.

"Hey," I said, doing my best to sound casual. "All fixed?"

"What an odd bunch," said Dad. "Not even a

thank you."

"You missed all the fun," said Mum. "What have you been up to?"

"Oh," I said, linking arms with my parents as we walked back to the Gold-Wing.

"Nothing much."

…And that is the story of how I, Sally Comet, sent the space pirates packing across the galaxy – with a little help from Pharaoh Varden Kar the Third!